GUIDE TO MAPLE TAPPING
Second Edition

Guide to Maple Tapping
Second Edition

Also by Julie Fryer:

How to Open & Operate a Financially Successful Small Farm
(Atlantic Publishing 2014) co-authored with Melissa Nelson

Growing Peppers: Clover's Home and Garden Guide to Gardening
(Clover's Home and Garden Publisher 2013)

The Complete Guide to Water Storage (Atlantic Publishing 2012)

The Teen's Ultimate Guide to Making Money When You Can't Get a Job
(Atlantic Publishing 2012)

The Complete Guide to Your New Root Cellar (Atlantic Publishing 2011)

Illustrator and Graphic Designer:
Michelle White
www.mmwgraphicdesign.com

Photography: Julie Fryer

Some photos have been reprinted from Federal Government websites
including the National Park Service and the USDA.

Guide to

MAPLE TAPPING

Second Edition

A Tree to Table Handbook for the Maple Tapper

by Julie Fryer

Contents

CHAPTER FOUR

More than Sugar Maples...59

CHAPTER FIVE

Cooking Ideas and Recipes...69

CHAPTER SIX

Additional Resources...79

CHAPTER SEVEN

A Few Final Notes...81

Bibliography...85

Notes and Comments...87

Introduction

Welcome to the world of sugarmaking. It's the art of tapping sugar maple trees and making pure maple syrup. Collecting this sweet sap has stretched back for hundreds, maybe even thousands, of years. It's an age-old practice that has changed very little since the first tap was pounded into a tree – the tools have become modernized but the process is the same. It can't be rushed, you can't get a "jump start" on the season, and the finished product has the same sweet flavor as it did in colonial times. How many other modern-day hobbies can make that claim?

Tapping trees is a great family activity and fun for all ages.

We've written this book because we love maple tapping and want to share our knowledge with other folks thinking about taking up the hobby. As a child, I helped tap the maple trees on my Grandfather's farm in Michigan. Those fond memories inspired me to continue that family tradition with my own children.

I'm not the only one rediscovering this fun, nature-centered activity. Similar to the resurgence in vegetable gardening and other back-to-nature hobbies, more and more people are venturing into their backyards to tap maple trees. Nature centers and community education groups throughout the Northeastern and Midwestern USA, and Southern Ontario and Quebec, Canada, are hosting maple tapping days in an effort to get families back outside. The enthusiasm from kids and adults alike has helped grow interest in the fascinating and fun process of sap to syrup. Everyone loves the flavor of sweet maple syrup, but when they tap it themselves it becomes something really special.

Your sweet reward after the maple tapping season.

No book about maple tapping would be complete without mentioning what pure maple syrup is not. It is not that stuff found in a plastic bottle in the pancake aisle at the supermarket! Without exception, those products are made from corn syrup, artificial coloring, thickeners, and maple flavoring. Yuck! Take a quick look at the packaging and you'll find the producers can't even call it maple syrup. It's called "pancake syrup." Of course, those versions cost much less than the real deal, which is why most shoppers go for the plastic bottle. Since you'll be making your own, though, you won't need to worry about that!

Besides being a maple tapping enthusiast, I run an Illinois-based chain of retail garden shops called Clover's Garden Center. A focus of that business is to encourage people to get outside and in touch with nature. We have programs for first-time gardeners to help them through an initial season of vegetable and herb gardening. When discussing those programs, I often find myself referencing the "first crop of the season," which is, of course, maple sap. People's interest in trying maple tapping is always high, but they have little knowledge on how to begin. To help ease their way, I put together a variety of "Maple Tapping Kits" to get them going. The kits provide the best tools for tapping and include everything a maple tapper needs to get started.

Sap flows out of the spile as soon as it's inserted.

Though the tapping kits' equipment and instruction sheets helped make an initial season easy, people still seemed to have more questions about maple tapping. Hence, the idea for this book: one that is full of great information to help advance hopeful maple tappers to the land of warm maple syrup on pancakes!

To make it really fantastic, I teamed with a talented professional named Julie Fryer. She has much writing experience, authoring outdoor-focused how-to books about everything from building a root cellar to growing a garden to conserving rainwater. Julie also has a family tradition of maple tapping in Minnesota. She gathered the most current info; combined it with our personal experiences; and visited with large-scale sugarmakers, small tapping farms, and everyday folks who tap a few trees. She gathered these tips and tricks and put it all into this Guide to Maple Tapping. At first, the process may seem to require a lot of steps and directions — but once you've tapped your first tree and boiled down your first batch of syrup, you're on your way to a lifelong hobby.

This book will get you started, send you through the first season, and be a lifelong tapping guide for your family to have on the bookshelf. In no time, you'll be the one teaching others how to tap the sugarbush. So read on, head outside, and become a maple tapper!

Happy Tapping,

Jim Kuehnle

P.S. Please visit www.mapletapper.com for even more maple tapping information. We are growing an online community of friendly maple tappers who exchange ideas, tapping stories, tips, and tricks about our exciting hobby. Please use it as a resource for answers to questions, problem solving, access to tapping supplies, and great how-to photos and videos.

If you'd like to take a peek at our tapping kits, they can be found through these links:

**Sap Sack Kit:
http://www.mapletapper.
com/sap-sack-maple-
tapping-kit-book/**

Bucket and Spile Combo:
http://www.mapletapper.
com/bucket-spile-maple-
tree-tapping-kit-book/

**Tap Ten Trees Taps and
Tubes Kit:** http://www.
mapletapper.com/tap-ten-
trees-maple-tapping-kit-
taps-tubes-book/

CHAPTER ONE

What is Maple Tapping All About?

North America is the only place on Earth where you can collect pure maple sap. Although folks on other continents tap similar trees to collect sap, true maple sap is native only to this continent. Maple syrup and maple sugar are among the oldest agricultural commodities produced in the United States and Canada, dating back to the indigenous peoples of these areas. Some historians estimate that maple syrup and maple sugar made up nearly 12% of the diet of some Northeastern Native American tribes. When colonists first arrived, they found fully managed maple groves and a thriving maple sugar trading industry. From their carefully tended sugarbush, these original sugarmakers produced enough maple syrup and maple sugar to feed their people and trade with the

Native Americans used hollowed out logs to hold their sap and dropped in hot rocks to boil it down. *Photo courtesy of National Park Service.*

new arrivals. As with many North American crops, they also taught the colonists how to collect, cook, and use this sugary substance. With white sugar nowhere to be found, this must have been quite a sweet treat for those arriving in this strange, new wilderness.

Just a Few Facts

Where is maple syrup produced? Fourteen northern states from Minnesota to New York have thriving maple syrup industries. Vermont is the leader pouring out 42% of U.S. sales. Four Canadian provinces also contribute their share with Quebec producing nearly 70% of the world's maple syrup.

How many trees are tapped each year? It's estimated that commercial producers tap over 11.4 million trees per year.

How much syrup is made each year? Commercial sugarmakers in 2014 produced 3.17 million gallons of pure maple syrup. That's enough to fill over 70,000 bathtubs! No one knows for sure how much syrup is made by home hobbyists.

How much does pure maple syrup cost? Average price after the 2014 season was $37.40 per gallon making it a very valuable food commodity indeed.

When produced and sold by a commercial tapper, syrup is graded against rigorous USDA standards which were revised in 2015 to better align with international grading systems. These standards include a required Brix scale measurement of no more than 68.9% (this indicates the sugar content); good flavor and odor; intensity of flavor according to color; and clarity with no sediment or cloudiness. Syrups meeting all of these standards are then furthered classified within the Class A grade according to color:

- Grade A Very Dark (strongest maple flavor)

- Grade A Dark (robust maple flavor)

- Grade A Amber (a lighter but full-bodied maple flavor)

- Grade A Golden (mildest, most delicate maple flavor)

A fifth class of syrup used in food manufacturing is called "Processing Grade" and is typically darker and more robustly flavored than these four other grades. This syrup does not meet the Class A standards but still is acceptable as a food additive.

Beyond the sweet maple flavor, chemists have found 300 different flavor compounds in maple syrup. While not all are present in the same syrup, everything from a buttery flavor to a hint of coffee can be detected in certain batches. These differences are created by the many factors that affect the sap – such as soil quality and composition in the maple grove; time of the season and time of day that sap is collected; the type of tree, its genetics, and its health during the summer growing season; the temperatures during collection and storage; and finally, the process used to boil down the sap.

Maple Syrup is Hip

Some sugarmakers have taken maple syrup to a whole new level even going so far as to hire professional sommeliers to blend their syrups and batch their production much like they do with wine to create different "tasting" notes. Maple-inspired drinks, main courses, desserts, and more are showing up in five-star restaurants and maple syrup even made an appearance in the 2013 Presidential Inaugural Luncheon. That recipe is included in the recipe section in the back of this book.

While it may seem daunting to a beginner, making maple syrup is not difficult or complicated and there is plenty of room for error. Even a batch that's boiled a bit too long turns into delicious maple sugar! The entire process requires minimal tools and is an activity the entire family can enjoy. Other than the moving and pouring of boiling sap, every step of the process can be done together with your children or grandchildren. Probably the biggest commitment in making syrup is the time required during the days of sap collecting and the lengthy boiling process.

While filling your pantry with homemade syrup makes it all worthwhile, the real benefit is the time spent with your family, friends, or neighbors. After being cooped up indoors all winter, you'll have a great excuse to get outdoors and harvest the first crop of the season. You can share a festive and memorable experience with your pals, parents, kids, or grandkids (which they will certainly brag about to their friends.) You will all be taking part in one of North America's oldest hobbies. Best of all, maple tapping lets us all participate in a zero-electricity activity and the process of tapping certainly encourages ecological awareness. Years from now, you and your fellow sugarmakers will have tales to tell about your experiences at the sugarbush.

Mostly water, the first drop of the season flows out of the spile.

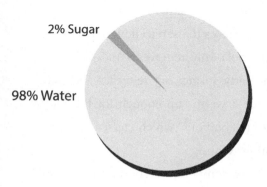

2% Sugar

98% Water

A Sappy Story

During the growing season, maple trees produce sugar inside their leaves through photosynthesis. Sap is a mixture of this sugar and the water absorbed through the tree's root system. The more leaves a tree has, the more sugar it produces to feed the tree and keep it healthy. Straight out of a tree, sap is 98% water and 2% sugar!

In the fall, as the days shorten and temperatures drop, the tree stops growing and begins to go into dormancy. Some of this sugar is trapped in the leaves which is why maple trees give the most vibrant fall colors. Leftover sap also remains in the tree and freezes in the outer "sapwood" layer of the tree.

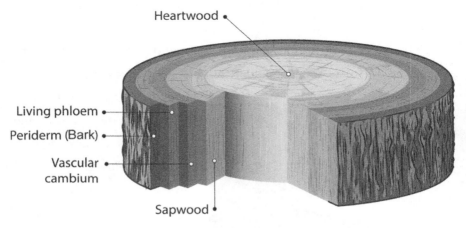

Anatomy of a tree trunk.

When spring finally comes around and the days begin to warm up, the tree once again requires nourishment and the sap thaws out and begins to run through the tree. When you tap a tree, you're accessing the sap's pathway. The release of that pressure near the taphole causes the sap to flow out into your bucket instead of up the tree. One taphole only removes 10% of the tree's sap for just a few weeks. During the early spring, sap refreezes and thaws numerous times within the tree – once it warms up enough for the sap to run continuously, it will cause the tree to "bud out" which creates sap with a buddy-flavor that makes for poor tasting syrup.

So, sugarmakers look for freeze/thaw temperature conditions to signal when they should start and stop tapping or collecting sap. The best scenario is: below freezing at night (preferably in the 20s°F) and above freezing during the day (preferably in the 40s°F.) This process is much more complex than described here and involves some pretty interesting science your kids would love! For more details, visit http://www.massmaple.org/sap.php for a helpful article on what makes sap flow. And not to worry, the tiny little hole you'll be making in the tree will easily heal and cause no damage to the tree.

How Sap Flows

During the day as temperatures warm up, positive pressure is created within the tree causing the sap to flow. If the tree is tapped, this pressure is released and sap is forced out through the taphole.

When temperatures drop below freezing at night, negative pressure or suction, is created which draws water into the tree through the roots and slows down the sap flow.

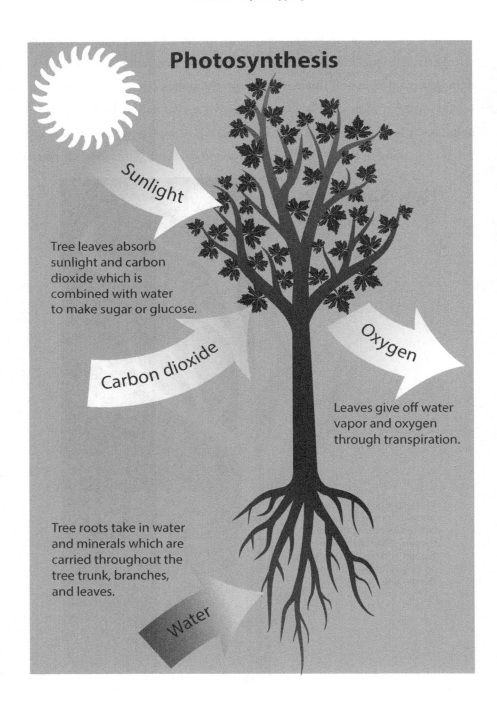

Photosynthesis

Sunlight

Tree leaves absorb sunlight and carbon dioxide which is combined with water to make sugar or glucose.

Carbon dioxide

Oxygen

Leaves give off water vapor and oxygen through transpiration.

Tree roots take in water and minerals which are carried throughout the tree trunk, branches, and leaves.

Water

The amount of sap each taphole will produce varies greatly depending on the tree, the time of year, environmental conditions such as the weather and soil conditions, and even at what point you are in the tapping season. Normally, a single taphole produces from a quart to a gallon of sap per flow-period (which can last a few hours or more than a day.)

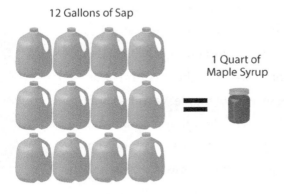

12 Gallons of Sap

1 Quart of
Maple Syrup

Over the season, you can expect approximately 10- to 12-gallons of sap per taphole. Most sugarmakers expect a 40-to-1 ratio in syrup production – after evaporation, 40 gallons of sap would concentrate down to one gallon of syrup. Sometimes you'll get lucky, though, and get 30-to-1. With this ratio in mind, you'd need four tapholes to end up with one gallon of syrup for the season. Now you can see why it's so expensive!

Sap collected over a 24-hour period in the Sap Sack.

Pure Sweetness

Because of the way it's collected and processed, maple syrup is considered all natural and organic. Nothing is added from tap to bottle – it's naturally gluten-, dairy-, and nut-free. However, if sap is collected from trees that have been chemically treated, the syrup cannot be considered organic. This is not recommended anyway because the chemicals would result in a bad tasting syrup.

The Next Big Thing: Maple Water

Proving once again that sugarmakers are always thinking, they've come up with a new product even in this established industry. Bottled Maple Water has hit the market and many are predicting it will eclipse the super-popular coconut water in the "health water" market. An eight-ounce serving of maple water has only 6 grams of sugar which is much less than comparable sports drinks. Taken straight from the tree with normal tapping methods, the sap is filtered, pasteurized, and packed aseptically in cardboard cartons. Nothing is added to the finished product. Maple water has all the nutrients and health benefits of maple syrup and it keeps a slightly sweet maple flavor. Try making your own maple water at home – just collect it, filter it, and boil it a bit to kill any bacteria. Let cool, keep refrigerated, and drink it straight or use as a base for tea or coffee.

Finished maple syrup is considered a "sucrose" with small amounts of glucose and fructose – so those watching their sugar intake must treat it as a sugar. However, unlike refined white sugar, maple syrup does contain minerals, vitamins, amino acids, and other compounds that make it slightly more nutritious than plain sugar.

Nutritional Facts

Minerals: calcium, potassium, manganese, magnesium, phosphorus, iron
Vitamins: B2 (riboflavin), B5 (pantothenic acid), B6 (pyridoxine), PP (niacin), biotin and folic acid.
Calories: 52 calories per tablespoon, 13.5 grams of carbohydrates, 0.1 grams of fat

The Process

With the science of how sap runs and the fussiness of the finishing process, you might think sugarmaking is best left to the pros. Naturally, you'll need to know certain details, but overall it's a simple activity that's easy to learn. The best part is that the finished product is such a sweet reward! The following sections will cover all the information needed to walk you through the process so nothing is left to chance. The good news here is that once you've assembled your supplies and tapped a tree, you're halfway to being a pro. You'll have the tools and the knowledge you need to tap trees for years to come. So let's get started on becoming a sugarmaker!

Supplies

Look online or visit a maple syrup farm and you'll notice a wide range of supplies used for tapping and cooking. Tappers are resourceful folks and have concocted all kinds of DIY devices to collect, boil, and finish their syrup. This approach to tapping is perfectly fine but for the beginner, this trial-and-error method can lead to loss of a whole season's batch. Unless you have a great mentor willing to share his or her secrets – or you've been through a few seasons – it's best to start out with pre-made tools and supplies. These supplies are fairly inexpensive and can be used for many seasons, making them well worth the upfront cost. Skimping on an important tool, such as using a flimsy evaporator pan, could mean the loss of your entire tapping effort. Just make sure you order everything well in advance of the season as they do sell out quickly. Cooking and bottling supplies will be covered in Chapter 3.

Some of these tools are a necessity, such as the drill, while others just make the job easier and more enjoyable. As with any outdoor activity, think safety first. Always tell someone when and where you'll be in the woods – and when you're expected back. Watch your step in the woods as the ground could be slick, practice good power tool use, and wear proper clothing to keep you warm and dry. To make the job easier, carry your tools and supplies in a bucket, apron or backpack. And once you're out in the woods, take some time to savor the experience and enjoy your surroundings.

Copy this Tapping Trick

A pro sugarmaker from Wisconsin told us he used a carpenter's apron to hold his drill, hammer, and spiles making it easy to carry tools from tree-to-tree. Pick up a few aprons at your local hardware store and make some for the whole family. Your kids will love having their own "work apron."

General Tools

- **Drill, 5/16" sharp drill bit, and permanent marker.** A well-charged cordless drill works best but you can also use an old-fashioned hand drill (sometimes called a hand brace or breast drill.) Mark the bit at 1½-inches from the end so you'll know when to stop drilling.

- **Small hammer or mallet.** Good for pounding in spiles or attaching and removing bucket lids.

- **Safety glasses.** Protects your eyes from wood shavings during drilling.

- **Clean Rags and Jug of Water.** Just in case you drop a spile or tubing into the mud!

- **GPS or Cell Phone.** This can help you find your way to your trees or call for help when deep in the woods.

- **Sturdy Boots or Snowshoes and Outdoor Gear.** Springtime means deep wet snow, gooey mud, and slippery leaves so you'll need proper footwear and clothing to get around.

- **ATV, Snowmobile, or Sturdy Sled with Runners.** Great for accessing remote trees or hauling back your buckets of sap.

- **Food-safe buckets or large jugs, preferably with removable lids.** These will be your collection devices at each tree (if you're not using an all-in-one system) and will also serve as the transfer bucket you carry from tree-to-tree to gather the collected sap. Buckets or jugs must be clean – but not washed with dish soap – and completely odor-free.

Tubing is threaded through the lid before inserting the spile in the tree.

Tapping Supplies

As mentioned earlier, there are many different types of tapping supplies available on the market. This book will highlight three of the most popular – they're preferred because they're easily moved, lightweight, and reusable from year to year. Each of these systems comes thoroughly assembled and

Example of the blue 5/16" spile used with the Bucket and Spile Combo Kit.

with complete directions included in the packaging, so we'll just highlight the features of each here. Additionally, more pictures and product details are available by visiting the online links listed in the Introduction and Resources section.

In this book, you'll hear a lot of talk about the "spile" – this is the official name for the tap or spout which is placed in the tree. Previous generations of sugarmakers used a 7/16" spile but research in the last decade has shown that a 5/16" spile causes less damage to the tree, allows for faster taphole healing, and does not reduce the sap yield when used with gravity systems such as tubing or buckets. After seeing this research and using the 5/16" spile ourselves, we've decided to stick with this one size. So when we assembled our full tapping kits, we sought out only the "tree saver" spile and, happily, we were able to find that size for all three of our tapping systems.

Large scale sugarbush with multiple, connected taplines.

All of the following tapping systems work well for the hobbyist tapper and are very easy to attach to the tree, empty, and clean for later use. For larger operations you might want to consider a tubing system running from tree-to-tree that ends in a large central collection device or a vacuum system which moves the sap more quickly.

Sap Sack System. This system includes four components: a heavy duty

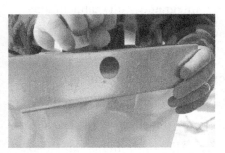

Sap Sack all assembled and ready to hang on the spile.

stainless steel spile, galvanized steel sack holder, a detachable metal ring to secure the bag in the holder; and heavy-duty, blue plastic, food-grade bags. The assembled holder hangs directly on the spile and is easily removed for emptying. The spile is interchangeable with other collection systems and the large bags can be washed and reused. The Sap Sack is handy because it's an all-in-one system and once the season is over, it takes up very little room for storage. *Tip: Assemble your sack and holders before going into the woods – much easier to do in a warm, dry kitchen! Also when emptying the filled sack into your bucket, leave the sack in place on the holder for stability.*

Bright blue tubes show up well against tree bark.

Tree Saver Tap and Spile Combo. These come pre-assembled with a heavy-duty plastic spile attached to a 36-inch length of blue plastic food-grade tubing designed for maple tapping. All components are washable and reusable but you will need to provide your own collection bucket or jug. These are also handy because they can be doubled up into one bucket or attached to each other through a coupler. Also, the bright blue color really stands out in the forest, making it easy to find your taps. *Tip: Be sure your tubing reaches your collection device once the spile is placed in the tree – measure before you drill. Also, account for snow melt which may lower your bucket's height.*

Bucket and Spile Combo. This kit includes a heavy-duty plastic spile

Integrated lid keeps the bucket covered.

with integrated lid attachment system and a large, light-blue bucket for visibility in the woods. It also offers all-in-one convenience and the bucket is super easy to remove and pour out into your transfer bucket. All components are also quite durable and should last for your sugarmaking career. *Tip: Don't be tempted to preassemble the lids and spiles – it makes it too hard to insert the spile in the tree and the lids are easy to assemble once the spile is in place.*

Rinse all equipment thoroughly with clean tap water.

Keeping it Clean

Because sap is basically water and sugar, it's the perfect breeding ground for bacteria, yeast, and other microorganisms. While these will all be boiled away and are not harmful to your health, they will eat the sugars in your sap which will affect your syrup's taste. The best way to prevent these from growing is to keep your operations as clean as possible – starting with clean equipment, keeping everything sanitary while tapping and cooking, and putting everything away in clean, dry condition. However, don't reach for the liquid dish soap just yet!

Remember that whatever is present in your sap will be concentrated down 40 times into your syrup. Even a miniscule trace of lemon-scented soap can create a bad tasting syrup – avoid scented detergents or iodine-based

Run clean water through tubing to remove all sap residue.

dairy cleaners. Instead, use the old standby cleaning agent, household bleach. Mix one part of unscented, regular household bleach (not commercial strength) with 20 parts hot water and scrub your equipment thoroughly. To clean tubing, force this solution through the entire tube while plugging one end. Be sure the tubing is filled and let it sit in the tube for a day or two. Thoroughly rinse your equipment so no traces of bleach remain.

Rinse again with fresh water at the beginning of the next season. When using tubing, some producers allow the first day's sap to run onto the ground just to ensure the bleach is removed.

Make sure your equipment is also in tip-top shape and do not use rusty or stained spiles, tubing, or buckets. If you're using new spiles, dip them in the above-mentioned bleach solution or drop them in boiling water to sanitize them before your first use.

When to Tap

The tapping season varies from region to region but generally starts in early March and lasts until mid-April. As mentioned earlier, when the sap starts and stops running depends greatly on day and nighttime temperature fluctuations. Sap flows most freely on days when a rapid warming trend in early to mid-morning (in the 40°F and above range) follows a cool, below freezing night (preferably in the mid 20s°F). Sap will still run outside of these ranges but may take longer to start running during colder snaps or "tap out" during continued warm spells.

Fuzzy buds start to open, signaling the end of tapping season.

Remember, once a tree buds out, the tapping season is over and the taps should be removed. Do not be tempted to tap your trees early to get a head start! This could crack the tree and because sap is mostly water, it will only freeze in the tap which can break your spile and possibly damage the tree.

Finding a Maple Tree

Hard maples (acer saccharum) are the best trees to tap because their sap has the highest sugar content of 2% to 3%. Also called sugar maple or rock maple, these trees produce the most flavorful and sweetest syrup. You can also tap soft maples, red maples, and boxelder but the sap has lower sugar content and a less robust, sometimes bitter flavor. These trees are covered in more detail in Chapter Four.

Maple tree just starting to turn colors. *Photo courtesy of NRCS/USDA.*

The best way to identify a sugar maple is to use an illustrated tree reference book or check online such as the USDA website – maple trees all have the same characteristics with slight and subtle variations between each subspecies of tree. Here are a few common but distinctive features that all maples share (with a few tips to help distinguish hard maple from soft maple):

- "Helicopter" seeds (technically called samaras) with two v-shaped wings that flutter down and away from the tree in the spring like the rotors on a helicopter. Hard maples drop seeds in the late summer or early fall and soft maples drop seeds in spring and early summer.

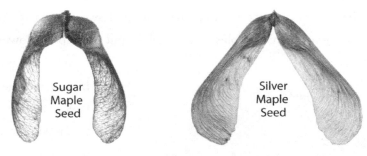

Seed photos courtesy of USDA.

- Separately lobed, pointy leaves with 3 to 9 veins per lobe, and a "U" shaped valley between the leaf segment. Sugar maple typically has 5 lobes.

Hard or Sugar Maple trees have darker green leaves with "smoother" points and the most vivid fall colors.

Soft or Silver Maple Trees have a lighter yellow-green color, much pointier leaves, a white or silver underside, and mostly yellow fall colors.

Sugar or Hard Maple Bark.

Silver or Soft Maple Bark. *Photo courtesy of the USDA.*

- Mature trees will have a dense, round canopy and can grow to be more than 80-feet tall. Sugar maples have light to dark gray bark with narrow, deep furrows while soft maples have a more layered, flaky bark.
- In the fall, sugar maple trees typically have the most colorful red, orange, or yellow leaves.
- Sugar maples are most prevalent in southern Canada, the Upper Midwest, the Northeastern states, and down the eastern seaboard of the United States. Sugar maples can be grown outside these areas but require climates with a freeze/thaw cycle to produce tasty sap.

U.S. Geological Survey map showing North American distribution of the sugar maple tree (acer saccharum.)

Picking the Best Trees to Tap

If possible, visit your tapping woods in the summer or fall as it will be easier to identify which trees are maples just by looking at the leaves. Tie brightly-colored marking tape around your trees (sometimes called flagging tape, available online or at most hardware or home improvement stores),

place a flag near your tree, or mark the tree location with your GPS. In the early spring when the trees don't yet have leaves, these markers will make it easier to find your sugar maples.

The key to good-tasting syrup is starting with a healthy tree! Look for a full canopy of leaves

Use weather resistant marking tape to mark trees in summer or fall.

extending downward – remember, the leaves create the sugar so the more leaves on the tree in the summer, the sweeter and more abundant the sap

will be in the spring. Trees with broken branches or significant leaf loss may not produce large quantities or flavorful sap. Also avoid trees that have been treated with pesticides or herbicides as this can be unhealthy for consumption and will most likely negatively affect the flavor.

Easy access makes collecting sap much more fun.

As you're choosing trees, also consider access and keep in mind that you'll be walking through mud or snow during the tapping season. The best case scenario is tapping trees right in your own yard, along a roadway, or on a path through the woods – even better if it's wide enough for a snowmobile or ATV. Also, you'll need to visit these trees daily and carry collected sap back to your vehicle or sugar shack – a remote stand of trees will make it more difficult to gather your sap.

Choose a tree that is at least 12" in diameter measured at 4½-feet above the ground. Larger trees can handle more than one tap but never put more than six taps on one tree. As a beginner, be sure you can handle the quantities that multiple taps will produce and that you have the time and space required to boil it all down.

Measure the diameter of your tree – basically the width of the tree as shown here.

Taps per Diameter Guide

12"- 18" diameter = 1 tap

18" - 32" diameter = up to 3 taps

32" or more diameter = up to 6 taps

Does Tapping Hurt the Tree?

Consider that the tiny little taphole is a very minor portion of the overall tree's body. It will readily heal much like when you sustain a small cut. If the tree is healthy when tapped and proper tapping procedures are followed, the taphole will start healing within weeks of the spile's removal and will continue to close up during the growing season. Many maple tree farms have been tapping the same trees for over 100 years. One thing to note: the bottom 4- to 6-foot "tapping zone" will result in trees that are less valuable if cut down for lumber.

Mark your drill bit at 1 ½" from the end so you'll know when to stop drilling.

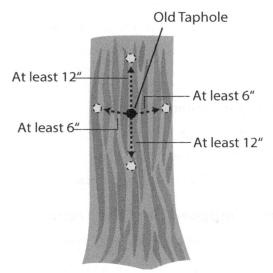

Old Taphole

At least 12"

At least 6"

At least 6"

At least 12"

Choosing a spot to drill a new taphole.

Drill steadily at a slight angle upwards.

Locating and Drilling the Taphole

As mentioned earlier, use a drill with a sharp, 5/16" drill bit marked at 1½-inches from the end. Select a spot on your tree above a large root or below a large branch as that's where the sap is headed to or from, and the route past your tap will be more direct. If possible, choose the south-facing side of the tree so the sun can warm up the tree and get the sap flowing better.

Locate the taphole approximately 2- to 4-feet up from the ground but make sure your tubing will reach your collection device. If using a bucket or jug sitting on the ground, be sure to take into account the snow depth and make sure your tubing will reach the bucket after the snow underneath it melts. If the tree has been tapped before, put the new tap no closer than 12" above or below an old tap mark or 6" from side to side of the old mark.

Stabilize yourself so you can be sure to hold the drill steady. Drill at a slightly upwards angle into the tree, stopping when you hit the mark on your drill bit. This ensures that you will only drill into the sapwood and not the heartwood, which could render the tree more susceptible to disease. Be careful not to wobble the drill – this can result in an "ovaled" hole

Cream-colored shavings from a newly drilled taphole.

which will not adequately hold the spile and allow sap to leak out around the edges. As you remove the drill, try to pull with it the debris left in the hole.

Shavings should be a light, creamy color – dark brown shavings indicate an undesirable tree. Use a pipe cleaner to remove any debris from the taphole. If needed, find a log to practice drilling before you try the real thing.

You will most likely see sap dripping from the hole as soon as you remove the drill. Place your spile in the hole with the spout facing outward, do not force it in, and gently tap on the spile to tighten it up in the tree.

Spile being placed in newly drilled taphole.

Do not tap on the spout itself as plastic spiles may crack. When the hammer begins to bounce back, you know you're at the end of the hole. If you go too far you could hurt the tree; if you don't go far enough the sap will leak out around your tap. When done, the spile should be snug enough that you cannot pull it out by hand but not too tight that it's cracking the bark. Once your spile is in, place your sack, bucket, or jug to collect the sap and let it run!

Sap begins running even before spile is fully inserted.

Bucket is hung on spile's hook and sap starts accumulating.

Place collection container on a level, non-slippery surface.

Be sure tubing will reach into bucket before drilling the hole.

Collecting your Sap

If you're using a system such as the spile and tube combo, you'll need to place a bucket or jug on the ground to collect your sap. Make sure the bucket is placed on level ground without a lot of leaves or snow underneath it. Once the bucket gets full it could slip and turn over, spilling your sap. Be sure your tubing reaches well into the bucket and is on a downhill, straight path to your bucket.

If the tubing is kinked, sagging, or crooked, sap can accumulate within the tube which can allow bacteria to grow in a spot that is very hard to clean. Thread your tubing through a hole in a closed lid so debris, insects, or rain do not get into the bucket. You might also want to secure your buckets or jugs to the tree with a bungee cord so heavy winds do not dislodge them.

The amount of sap collected each day will vary with the temperatures but you should check your equipment daily to make sure everything's in working order. Emptying the sap into a main collection

Empty sap each day into a main collection bucket and refrigerate until ready to boil.

Sap will sometimes freeze overnight if temperatures drop low enough. *Photo courtesy of the National Park Service.*

bucket – which you will then refrigerate or boil down – is also a daily task.

Sap left sitting in buckets, especially if the daytime temperatures stay well above 40°F, will cause bacteria to grow quickly. Refrigerated sap will also grow bacteria but at a much slower pace – that is why it's best to boil your sap within 24 hours of collecting it but you can hold it for four to five days if well chilled.

The best daily collection method is to take a large, food-grade bucket or buckets with handles to each tree and transfer the collected sap into the main bucket. Hauling these on a runner sled back to your sugar shack or vehicle will make life much easier. If using the Sap Sack system, be sure to leave the full bag in the holder while pouring. You will notice debris, insects, and other foreign objects in your sap. Do not despair, these will be filtered out! If it's turned really cold at night, you might also find a chunk of ice in your bucket or coming out of your spout – just gently remove it and throw out. And, be happy that Mother Nature has just removed some of the water from your sap so you should have it boil it less!

Can I freeze my sap to condense it?

Now this idea might have just occurred to you: wouldn't it be easier to simply freeze the water out? Native Americans and early settlers did sometimes use this method mostly because they did not have heavy-duty tools that would stand up to high heat. Folks are still experimenting with it and some large producers are beginning to use a "freeze concentration" method where the sap is slightly frozen as it travels through the pipes. There's more research to be done but the consensus is that preliminary freezing will work to reduce the water amounts but you still need to boil it for evaporation and to develop flavor and color through caramelization. Also, freezing can carry away a bit of the sugar so you will lose part of your overall harvest. Again, sugarmakers are ingenious so it doesn't hurt to try!

Once you get back home, give your sap its first filtering. For this step you can use a clean (with no laundry soap remnants) cotton t-shirt or a few layers of cheesecloth. Stretch over a bucket and slowly pour the sap through to seine out debris and other undesirables. Refrigerate the sap until ready to boil. Cooking and further filtering instructions are covered in Chapter 3.

End of Season Chores

You will know when the season is over – either the trees will bud out, the sap amounts will slow down greatly, or you'll reach your personal quota! Once you're done, use a claw hammer to gently pry the spiles out of the tree and wash them as described earlier in the chapter. Make sure all your equipment is completely dry and store it away until next season. Also be sure to check equipment for damage – most products will hold up well for multiple seasons but eventually may need replacement.

Spile easily pulls out with a little pressure.

CHAPTER THREE

Making Syrup

Now we get to the fun part! As mentioned earlier, there are many, many tools people have developed – mostly as DIY projects – to boil their sap down but the process remains the same. Boil and boil some more! Whatever it takes to get the water boiled out of your sap will work. However, the process goes more smoothly and the final product is much better, if you follow a few proven practices using the right tools.

Before we get any further into the boiling, let's talk safety. During this process, you will be working with fire or flammable gases and handling large quantities of boiling hot, sticky syrup. Please be careful, especially if children are helping you. Wear long sleeves, pants, and gloves to protect from splatters. Don't try to pour sap from large pans without help. Make sure you have a first aid kit and a bucket of water or hose nearby for emergencies.

Your entire goal right now is to remove the water from your sap and concentrate the sugars. The flavor of your finished syrup is created by the caramelization of the sugars during the boiling process. The longer the sap is boiled in the pan, the darker and stronger the flavors become. Along with the tree qualities and storage/collection issues mentioned earlier, the flavor can also be affected by the cleanliness of your boiling room and storage bottles. Stainless steel is the best choice for boiling and glass jars or bottles are the best for storage – we'll talk more about this later in the chapter. For now, we'll detail a few of the essential steps and the best tools needed and then walk you through the steps required to get your syrup finished.

Wood-burning stove with multiple evaporator pans. *Photo courtesy of the National Park Service.*

Space

You will be tempted to boil your sap down on the kitchen stove – be warned that everything around the pot will be sticky! Even the steam coming off your pot contains tiny bits of sugar which will joyfully attach to your walls, oven hood, and floor. Instead of dealing with a sticky mess, make a space for yourself outside or in a shed. You'll want some kind of overhead shelter in case it starts to rain or snow or the weather turns cold while you're boiling. You've probably heard the term "sugar shack" – a dedicated space for maple syrup making. Now's your chance to build your own!

Cooker and Fuel Source

The boiling down process will take many, many hours and greatly depends on how much sap you're starting with. You will need a way to cook your sap and choices include:

- A regular kitchen stove used outdoors – a gas flame is best because you can control the temperature better. This is also the best choice for the finishing stage of cooking.

- A single gas burner (such as those sold as a "turkey cooker") with a well-fitting pan.

- A wood fire built within a structure, such as cement blocks or freestanding wood stove, upon which your pan will sit.

Along with your chosen cooking methods, you'll need abundant fuel close to your cooking station – enough to last the many hours of boiling. Additionally, you'll need sufficient lighting in case your boiling or bottling goes past dark.

Evaporator and Boiling Pans

For a small-batch hobbyist the boiling process is less complex than for the commercial cooker. Large operations typically use a continuous-feed evaporator which continuously heats the sap, feeds it into another constantly-boiling evaporator pan, and then pours it off for finishing.

This is necessary because adding cold sap to a boiling evaporator pan will cause the whole batch's temperature to drop which will lengthen the boiling time.

Spout leading from prewarmer pan. It can be turned to pour into the larger evaporator pan during boiling.

Most hobbyist tappers use multiple pots and pans to re-create this three stage process:

1. The first batch of sap for the day is poured into the large evaporator pan, leaving at least 3" to 6" of headroom to prevent boiling over. If all the sap you have fits in your pan, you do not need to do Step 2.

2. Once the sap in the evaporator pan starts to boil and condense, you can start warming extra sap in your other smaller pans.

3. As this extra sap is heated to boiling, pour it into the larger pan remembering to leave headroom to prevent boil over. Continue this process until all your sap is in the large evaporator pan and boil the entire batch to the finishing point.

Multiple kettles used for prewarming and finishing.

Finally, as the sap nears the 216°F mark in the large evaporator pan, it's filtered and poured into a large kettle (usually the same kettle you used to prewarm it) and then put on a smaller heat source to finish it. This last step keeps the syrup from becoming too shallow in the pan which can lead to overheating or burning.

The rate at which the sap's water evaporates depends upon numerous factors such as: pan size and construction; type of heat source; and even the temperature of the sap being added to the evaporator. If using a shallow, rectangular pan with lots of surface area, it takes between 9 and

Commercial sugar shack with multiple warmer and evaporator pans. *Photo courtesy of National Park Service.*

18 hours to produce one gallon of syrup. With a deep, circular pan, it can take as little as 28 hours and as long as 56 hours.

Pre-made hobbyist sized evaporators can be bought online and these are nice to have because they typically have a spout for pouring out the syrup – instead of having to ladle it out by hand or try pouring from the large pan. However, it's not difficult to find pans or make your own. Look for a heavy-duty pan that can withstand prolonged heat – preferably a large, flat pan with sides at least 6- to 8-inches high to prevent boiling over. Many commercial kitchen supply stores sell large, flat roasting pans for a relatively inexpensive price. You can also find older enamelware or stainless steel pans at auctions, yard sales, or online trading sites – just be sure they are spotless and not corroded or rusty. Regular, quality, heavy-bottomed large kettles also work and are handy for use in the preheating and final stages of boiling.

Building your own wood "stove" is fairly simple and does not require any special skill. Look online for "cement block evaporator plans" and you will find hundreds of ideas. Better yet, visit with another tapper and see how they've built their cooker. One of the tappers consulted for this book used his brother's metal working skills to build a cooker out of an old 55-gallon drum and an evaporator pan to fit the stove. The only requirement for your cooker is that it can sufficiently hold your pan 18- to 24-inches off the ground and above the fire.

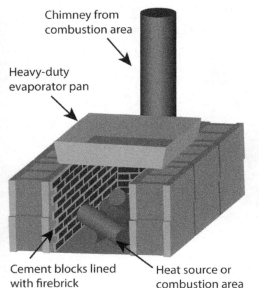

Chimney from combustion area

Heavy-duty evaporator pan

Cement blocks lined with firebrick

Heat source or combustion area

Moving hot sap off the fire to pour off into finishing pots.

Keep in mind, though, that whatever system you invent, you will be pouring or moving boiling hot sugary substances out of it! If the pan is too unwieldy or large to move, you could risk serious burns or at least end up spilling your almost-finished syrup.

Filtering

Before you are finished you will filter the sap three times – you've already done the first filter when you brought it in from the woods and this filter can be made from cheesecloth or other cotton material that is clean and without laundry soap present. The second filtering occurs as you pour concentrated sap from the evaporator into the finishing pot.

The third and final filter is done after the sap has reached its finished temperature and is poured into bottles. These last two stages require food-safe filters made from felt or wool, Orlon, or other synthetic materials

designed to handle hot syrup. Do not use coffee filters as the pores are too small. Most maple suppliers sell a variety of filters designed for each step. They are reusable and will last for many seasons.

Hot sap is poured from the large evaporator pan into a filter suspended over the finishing pot. Within minutes it's filtered through and ready to continue boiling.

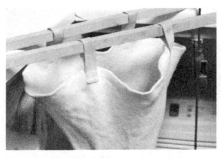

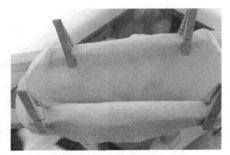

During the final filtering, syrup is poured through two filters clipped together. On the bottom is the heavier wool filter shown here hanging from dowels over another kettle.

The lighter filter is placed inside the wool filter and clipped together so it will stay in place once syrup is poured through.

This is not a step to be skimped on or skipped. The first stage of the filtering process obviously removes unwanted debris such as insects but the final two stages remove "sugar sand" which develops as the sap in concentrated and will affect your finished syrup's quality if left in the bottle.

Thermometer

You must use a thermometer that has a readable scale with each degree marked in the 200°F to 230°F range. This is the range at which your syrup will be finished (or turned into sugar) and it climbs past the optimal range quite quickly. Some candy thermometers will work as will newer electronic

thermometers with digital readouts. Look for a thermometer that has an attachment handle or clip so you do not have to hold it above the boiling syrup. If using a new thermometer or one that has been dropped, it's best to calibrate it so you know it's accurate.

Digital thermometer held over the pot of nearly-done boiling syrup.

Also, to really control the process, you should calibrate your thermometer each day as the barometric pressure can slightly alter the boiling point.

How to calibrate a thermometer:

1. Heat distilled water to a rolling boil.
2. Place your thermometer in the water making sure to have 2-inches of room on all sides and up from the bottom of the pan.
3. Temperature should read within +/- 2°F of 212°F (the boiling point of water.) If it's outside of this range, take note of the discrepancy or replace the thermometer. For instance, you're looking for a temperature of 219°F for finished syrup – if your thermometer is +3°F off, you'll know to boil it to 222°F (as shown on your thermometer.)

Be sure to clean your thermometer thoroughly without soap before and after each use.

Hydrometer and Cup

These are fairly inexpensive tools and will help you measure the density of your syrup. They will last forever if handled carefully. Syrup hydrometers

contain a Brix scale which measures the sugar content of a liquid. For maple syrup, you're looking for a 66% to 67% sugar content. Any lower and the syrup will be thin and prone to souring. Any higher and

Hydrometer hangs over the edge of the evaporator pan.

it will form sugar crystals. You can get by without using a hydrometer but they're nice to have if your syrup seems too thin or too thick. Hydrometer kits can be found through many online retailers and will include thorough directions on use and storage.

Kitchen Tools

As with most cooking or canning projects, you'll need general kitchen tools throughout the process. Assemble these before you start cooking:

- Heavy-duty, metal pan scrapers, long-handled slotted spoon, long-handled large ladle.
- Flavorless vegetable oil and eye dropper for finishing stage.
- Labels and markers for the finished bottles.
- Funnel for filling jars or dedicated, new electric coffee maker with pour spout.
- Clips or clothespins for holding filters.
- Glass canning jars or bottles with sealable lids. Make sure rims are not chipped.
- Clean kitchen towels and warm water for wiping up spills and cleaning bottles.
- Thicker towels for holding bottles while cooling.
- Table or work bench where bottles can sit undisturbed for 24 hours.
- Heat resistant gloves, long sleeve shirt, and long pants for protecting against splatters.
- Lots and lots of patience!

The Boiling Process

Once you have your tools gathered, your cooking station and bottling plan set up, and your sap collected, it's time to get down to business. Your goal is to heat the sap to that magic number of 219°F (or 7°F above water's boiling point.) It will take many hours to get within this range but the final few degree changes go quickly! We talked a bit about this three-step process already so here's a recap with more details.

Sap heated to a vigorous rolling boil.

Step 1: Beginning Boil

Pour filtered sap into your evaporator pan and start cooking it over high heat. Leave at least 3- to 6-inches of space between the sap and the top edge of the pan as it can foam up and boil over. If you have too much sap for your evaporator pan,

heat the remainder in small pots over high heat and add to the larger pan as the water boils away – remembering to keep headspace and at least 1½-inches of liquid in your pan to prevent burning. Continue this process until all your sap is boiling in one big batch. Keep your sap boiling as aggressively as possible – this creates a better quality syrup and speeds up the processing time.

Cooking Tip

One of our sugarmakers told us they keep a cup or so of unboiled sap reserved for "emergencies" during cooking. Sometimes the temperature will quickly spike during the finishing boiling stage – this reserved, cool sap can rescue a batch and lower the temperature before it turns into candy!

Step 2: Second Filter and Finish Boil

As your sap reaches the 216°F range, remove it from the main heat source and finish the boiling process in a smaller pan over a more controllable heat source such as a gas cooker. The temperature jumps quickly at this point and you must be able to control the heat so your syrup does not exceed 219°F. Once you go over that temperature there is no going back and you'll have sugar instead of syrup.

Heated sap is run through the second filtering into the finishing pot.

To transfer your sap to the finishing pot, first let the heat drop slightly by turning down the gas or shoveling away the hot coals until the syrup stops bubbling. Pour or ladle your syrup through your felt filter suspended over your cooking pot. It is very hot so be careful! Again, leave a few inches of headroom in the pot to avoid boil-overs. Do not put the empty evaporator pan back on the heat without water or sap left in it, as the pan will scorch and be very difficult to clean. Remove the filter, place your thermometer in the pan so it's not touching the sides or bottom, and continue the boiling process.

Full pot of nearly-done sap moved to the stove for the final boiling stage.

While it took many hours to get to this temperature, the next few degrees will jump quickly so you must keep a close eye on the batch until it's done. As it gets closer to that 219°F mark, it will take on an oily appearance and the bubbles will get smaller and closer together. Sap might also develop a foamy layer as it boils. Just skim it off with a large slotted spoon.

As sap boils, it will sometimes foam up. Just reduce heat a bit and skim off.

At this point, syrup can quickly boil over, so watch the level in the pot. If it starts to boil up, lower the heat. If this does not stop the boil-over, use the eye dropper to put one drop of vegetable oil in the pan. This breaks the surface tension much like a defoaming agent. If your batch goes over the target temperature, immediately remove it from the heat and add more unfinished sap to reduce the sugar concentrations. This sometimes works to rescue the batch and just resume the boiling process until you get back up to the proper temperature.

Once you reach 219°F, remove your syrup from the heat and cover it with a lid to keep the heat in. Now is the time to use your hydrometer kit to test the density and continue the boil if necessary – however, you still cannot boil your batch over the target temperature. The density shown on the hydrometer's Brix scale should be at least 66 Brix and no more than 67.5 Brix.

Step 3: Final Filter

Finished syrup is poured through the final filters.

It's natural to have some sediment in your finished syrup. This is called "sugar sand" or niter and it needs to be removed before bottling. If you filtered well during

Step 2, you might not have much remaining sediment. For this step use a two-step filter: the outside filter is a felt or wool cone and the inside filter is

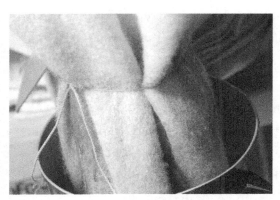

a thinner, synthetic Orlon syrup filter. Pour your syrup through this combo and into another pot to keep it hot while bottling.

After all syrup is poured into the filter, tie and squeeze to get out every last drop.

Hot syrup will filter quickly so handle carefully. Some people skip this step and just let the syrup sit in the refrigerator or snowbank for 24 hours so the sediment settles to the bottom – this does create more waste and you'll need to reheat your syrup before bottling it. Your filters are reusable and after you're done bottling, rinse the filters out with hot water (no detergent) and hang to dry.

Heating and Bottling Tip

One sugarmaker showed us how they use an electric coffee maker to keep syrup warm during bottling. Just position your final filters inside the prewarmed coffee

maker and pour in the hot syrup. The syrup will filter through, stay warm, and you can fill your jars from the spout!

Step 4: Bottling

After this last filtering, your syrup is ready to bottle. Syrup should be between 180°F to 185°F for bottling, so reheat your syrup if it's cooled down during the filtration process or has been refrigerated overnight. Start with

sterilized, hot jars and lids, wear a thick glove to protect your hand from the heat, and carefully pour or ladle syrup into each bottle to the top – as it cools the syrup will shrink in the bottle. Wipe the rims with a clean cloth, tighten the lid, and tip upside down so the hot syrup floods the container neck.

Full jar resting on its side.

Lay the jars or bottles on their sides for 24 hours – turning over once during this time. When cool, wipe the jars off and label with the date. Be sure to follow safe canning practices and keep a clean work space while bottling. After cooling, the syrup will shrink in the jar so don't be surprised when your filled jars suddenly have an inch of headroom!

Storage

Syrup will shrink in the bottle as it cools.

Properly bottled pure maple syrup should be stored in a cool, dry, dark place and will keep for up to one year. Maple syrup can also be frozen indefinitely – it will not harden, though, due to the high sugar content. Once opened, syrup should be stored in the refrigerator and used within six months of opening. If you notice any mold or discoloration, discard the contents as it may not be safe to eat. Also, do not store your syrup in plastic containers as the syrup may absorb odd flavors or odors from the plastic.

CHAPTER FOUR

More than Sugar Maples

As we talked about in Chapter One, photosynthesis is what helps produce sugar for the tree to feed on and this process is used by all trees. So, every tree has some "sugar" in its sap but not all of this sap is as delicious or as high in sugar content as maple sap. Many regions, though, without abundant sugar maples tap other trees to collect sap water, boil into

syrup, and further cook into candy or sugar. Each variety of tree sap will have a different flavor, color, and even sweetness but in general the process of tapping, collecting, filtering, and syrup making is the same.

Most sugarmakers who venture out to other tree types will admit that non-sugar maple syrup can be an acquired taste. With descriptions ranging from wild-tasting to bitter to earthy, expect something different if you decide to try making syrup from one of these trees.

Of course if it tastes good to you and you're willing to put in the time, then it's a worthwhile endeavor! As the sugaring industry has grown, folks have also started making blends of syrup from different tree types. This can lead to some really interesting flavors and colors and you'll definitely end up with one-of-a-kind syrup.

As with sugar maples, always select healthy trees, empty your buckets often, and remove taps as soon as buds appear. You can generally use the same equipment for all types of sap but some differences are needed in filtering and cooking equipment and those are mentioned in the following sections. Time and effort needed will be the biggest difference you notice with non-sugar maple sap. Because the sugar content is usually lower, you'll

need much more sap and longer boil times to produce the same quantity of finished syrup. For example, birch trees typically have a 100-to-1 sap to syrup yield so 100 gallons of sap yields one gallon of syrup.

This is nearly three times that of sugar maple sap which usually falls in the 30- to 40-to-1 range. That difference makes for more work in the field in tapping trees and hauling sap and more fuel and time required for boiling.

The season for sugaring is generally the same – some trees start later such as birch and some last longer such as walnut. The freeze/thaw cycle does affect how well sap flows but in more temperate regions such as the Western United States, trees can be tapped all winter as long as they're dormant. In all cases, sap will not produce good-tasting syrup if the tree is in bud or growing leaves.

Maple Family Trees

Throughout this book we've focused on Sugar Maples but as part of the maple family, Soft Maples and Boxelder trees also yield a sweet sap with relatively high sugar content. If you don't have a traditional Sugar Maple, try these varieties but the season may be shorter depending on your climate.

Black Maple (Acer nigrum): This variety most closely resembles a sugar maple and the two are often confused. Black Maple trees have a more limited range but the sap is nearly as sweet and abundant as a sugar maple.

Red Maple (Acer rubrum): Widely spread throughout North America, Red Maple is recognized as America's most common variety of tree and is known for its beautiful fall colors. This tree is also very suitable for tapping but the sap has a lower sugar content and the buds pop out sooner than sugar maple.

Silver Maple (Acer saccharinum): This fast-growing soft maple is also widely spread throughout North America. It, too, has lower sugar content (approximately 1.7% versus 2% of sugar maples) and the tree buds out earlier making for a shorter season. Finished syrup has a more earthy taste and will be lighter-colored and thinner.

Box Elder, also called Ash-Leaved Maple or Manitoba Maple (Acer negundo): Another hardy and fast-growing but short-lived maple variety, Box Elder sap has lower sugar content and syrup has a more sorghum-like flavor.

Norway Maple (Acer platanoides): Another tree similar to the sugar maple, the Norway Maple's sap is less sweet. This tree tolerates poor growing conditions and is now considered invasive in many parts of the United States.

Canyon Maple, also known as Big Tooth Maple (Acer grandidentatum): This tree is closely related to the sugar maple and is native to interior western North America. Its range extends from Western Montana to northern Mexico. Sugar content is higher than most maples but sap yield is much lower than sugar maples.

Bigleaf Maple (Acer macrophyllum): Another western native, Bigleaf Maples grow mostly along the Pacific coast from Alaska all the way to southern California. Sap has lower sugar content and less sap yield compared to sugar maples.

Rocky Mountain Maple (Acer glabrum): Also native to western North America, Rocky Mountain Maple sap has been used for centuries by Native Americans as a medicinal treatment for swelling and other general ailments.

Birch Trees

Likely the most common non-maple tree used for syrup, many varieties of Birch are tapped throughout North America and in regions such as Alaska where maple trees are not abundant. The Alaskans really ramped up Birch syrup production in response to World War I sugar shortages and they now have a thriving cottage industry, making everything from birch syrup to beer to wine to vinegar to soft drinks. Birch sap straight out of the tree is valued by many as a sweet spring tonic (much like mineral water) or as base for tea

and coffee. It's also bottled and sold commercially in Europe, China, Korea, Finland, and Russia. Finished birch syrup tastes more savory than sweet with rich body and hints of caramel, sorghum, honey, and even balsamic. These flavors may not pair well with pancakes but are great for marinades, dressings, meats, and veggies.

Birch sugarmaking differs in a few ways from maple sugaring. The sap run usually begins later in the year in early April, often at the end of the maple sugaring season. Daytime temperatures need to get into high 40°s and low 50°s with cold nights to get the sap flowing. Because of this late-season harvest and warmer weather, the sap spoils more quickly if left sitting all day in the buckets so birch sugarmakers often must collect sap twice per day. The season, too, is shorter and typically lasts for only two to three weeks. You can only use one tap per tree no matter what size the tree but choose a tree at least 10" in diameter. The sap itself is more acidic which can eat away at metal containers, leaving behind an unpleasant taste. So, you should only use plastic, nylon, stainless steel, or glass during tapping, collecting, cooking, and storage.

An interesting tidbit about birch trees: they share an essential oil with the wintergreen plant and this commonly-used natural flavoring is most often distilled from the tree and not the plant! Some of this wintergreen flavor will be retained in the syrup and many sugarmakers add birch twigs to the boiling sap right at the end to add this characteristic flavor.

Temperature Really Matters!

The predominant sugar in birch sap is fructose (as opposed to sucrose in maple sap) which gives it the lowest glycemic index of all sugars. The fructose, though, also means birch syrup scorches more easily and will darken more with boiling. For this reason, the cooking process is a bit more labor intensive than maple syrup cooking. Almost the exact opposite of how we make maple syrup, the birch sugarmaker has to go by sight to tell when the syrup is close to done. The thermometer does still matter – only because your goal is to keep the temperature under 200°F. Anything above that and your batch will burn and that's the end of it!

Because it's so finicky, most commercial producers use reverse osmosis for the majority of processing and only boil it at the end for flavor. You can cook it at home with your evaporator but it needs to cook at a lower temperature and at a much less aggressive boil. Most birch sugarmakers cook birch sap using a three step process:

1. Boil in a traditional evaporator until volume is reduced by half. Do not add sap to the batch as it cooks, though, as it can cause scorching of already-boiling sap.

2. Transfer this reduced sap to a smaller pan and cook at a low simmer. Keep the temperature below 200°F and do not let it boil. If it starts turning dark brown, remove from heat immediately. Continue this simmer until sap is reduced to about 25% of the original volume.

3. Transfer this sap to a crockpot and set temperature on low but leave the lid off so water can continue evaporating. This can also be done in a double boiler. Again, make sure the temperature does not go above 200°F. Continue cooking until syrup starts to thicken and turn golden amber. Finished birch syrup will not be as thick as pure maple syrup

but should read between 66 and 67 on the Brix scale. Be sure to filter it as you would with maple syrup and seal while hot in glass jars.

Any tree in the Betula family will produce birch sap but most prefer Paper Birch:

White Birch, also called Paper Birch or Canoe Birch (Betula papyrifera): The provincial tree of Saskatchewan and the state tree of New Hampshire, the white birch has half the sugar content of sugar maple sap but is considered the sweetest sap of all birches.

Yellow Birch (Betula alleghaniensis): The sap from this variety of birch has been found to have higher mineral composition and higher antioxidant value than sugar maple. Sap from the yellow birch is much lower in sugar content and the tree buds out sooner making for a shorter season. Finished syrup has a caramel-like flavor.

Black Birch, sometimes called Sweet Birch (Betula lenta): This tree is native to eastern North America and grows from Ontario to Georgia. The sap is most commonly used to make birch beer.

Other Trees

Call it desperation or ingenuity, the sugarmaking community is filled with tales of surprisingly tasty syrup made from unusual sources. Trees, such as Black Walnut, have been overshadowed by Maple but are now getting serious study as another valuable source of sap and syrup. Researchers are finding promise not only in a tasty end product but in another avenue for small agricultural markets. Because so little research exists, tapping these non-traditional trees is still somewhat of a trial-and-error experience. As a home hobbyist, it's an opportunity to be adventurous and try something new. Follow the same tapping and boiling process as you would with maple syrup. Note: anyone with nut allergies should avoid syrup made from nut-producing trees such as walnut or butternut.

Black Walnut (Juglans nigra) or Butternut (Juglans cinerea): Most commonly found in the Midwest and northeastern U.S., walnut and butternut tree syrup is darker than maple syrup with a more earthy, nutty flavor. The sap flow depends on the same freeze/thaw cycle and the season

begins at the same time. The length of the season, though, is sometimes a bit longer as these trees are often the last to bud out. You will notice that the color of the sap will darken over the season and the darker it gets, the more robust the finished syrup will taste.

Sugar content is similar to maple trees and you can expect a 40-to-1 sap to syrup yield. However, the amount of sap produced by the tree is typically about one-third less than sugar maple. The sap also contains more pectin than maple sap – the same type used to make jams and jellies so the sap is thicker and harder to filter and traditional thick, wool filters will not work. Try cheesecloth or a clean thin cotton dish towel. Walnut trees also have thicker bark which can be harder to drill through but trees can be tapped at a smaller diameter (8" versus 12"). The cooking process is exactly the same as maple syrup.

Sycamore (Platanus occidentalis): Found in southern Ontario and much of northern and eastern America, Sycamore tree sap has long been collected as drinking water and for syrup making. The tapping season and sugarmaking process are identical to maple trees and the sap-to-syrup ratio is similar. The flavor, though, is not the greatest and many considered this a "syrup of last resort" due to its almost-scorched taste. It can, though, be blended with other saps and will add a bit of butterscotch flavor when mixed with maple or other syrups.

Hickory (Carya genus): The Pecan tree is also part of this family and old-timers have tapped both types for their sap which is cooked down just like maple syrup. However, most "Hickory Syrups" sold today are not made from tree sap but instead from an extract taken from the bark and nut shells which is then combined with sugar and water to make syrup.

Give it a Try!

If you're interested in tapping some of these non-traditional trees, search online for forums discussing each tree. Sugarmakers love to share ideas and as more and more try out different saps and syrup making methods, the entire hobby benefits. It's also a great idea to pick up a tree identification book or check your local Extension office for more information on choosing trees in your area.

CHAPTER FIVE

Cooking Ideas and Recipes

Your first meal of homemade maple syrup just has to be a big stack of pancakes! This is what you worked for all season and it tastes so good. After you've had your fill of flapjacks – and still have a pantry full of pure maple syrup – you'll want to venture past the breakfast table.

For starters, maple syrup can easily be used as a replacement for sugar but obviously it will impart a maple flavor to your dish. Generally, one cup of pure maple syrup equals one cup of sugar and can be swapped out in most recipes. For cookies and cakes that also use liquid ingredients, just reduce the liquids by three tablespoons for each cup of maple syrup used.

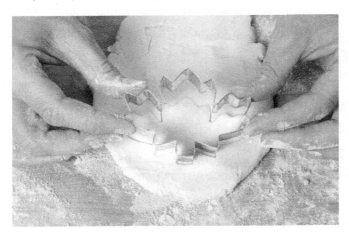

Cut the Sugar

Use maple syrup instead. One of our sugarmakers, Chantel Prigge, has found tasty ways to use her bounty. Try some of these yummy ideas in your kitchen:

- Pour on oatmeal, English muffins, or over cereal
- Make homemade dressing with maple syrup, balsamic vinegar, and sea salt
- Saute sweet potatoes, onions, peppers, and mushrooms for a lovely caramelization
- Instead of sugar water, can peaches or apples with maple syrup mixed with water instead. Then use the peach liquid to sweeten your tea or morning yogurt.

In the pioneer days, sugar was scarce but maple syrup was abundant – and those recipes are still good today. You can use already-bottled syrup for these recipes or make them during your initial boiling phase. Be sure, though, to calibrate your thermometer each time you boil syrup. Look at cooking stores or hobby stores for candy molds designed for hot liquids. These all make great gifts and are fun for the whole family:

- **Granulated Maple Sugar.** On a non-humid day, heat syrup to 252°F to 257°F (or 40°F to 45°F above the boiling point) and transfer immediately to a flat pan. Stir within this pan until it becomes granulated and all the moisture is gone. Sieve through a coarse screen (1/8-inch hardware screen) to create uniform granules. Use as a one-to-one white sugar replacement.

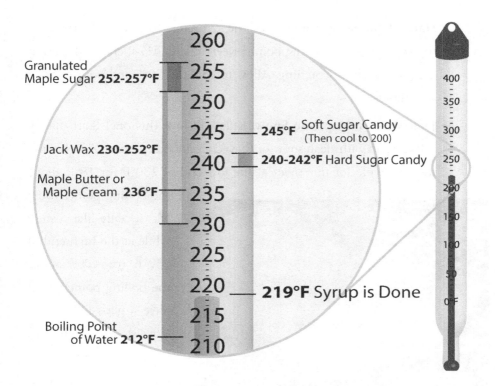

Granulated
Maple Sugar **252-257°F**

260

255

250

245 —— **245°F** Soft Sugar Candy
(Then cool to 200)

Jack Wax **230-252°F**

240 —— **240-242°F** Hard Sugar Candy

Maple Butter or
 Maple Cream **236°F** —— **235**

—— **230**

225

220 —— **219°F** Syrup is Done

215

Boiling Point
 of Water **212°F** —— **210**

400
350
300
250
200
150
100
50
0°F

• **Hard Molded Sugar.** Follow the same steps for granulated sugar but do not put through a screen. Instead pack into candy molds – be sure to

follow the manufacturer's directions on prepping and cleaning the molds.

• **Molded Soft Sugar Candy.** Heat syrup to 245°F (or 33°F above the boiling point,) pour into a flat pan, and allow to cool undisturbed to 200°F but no lower than 160°F. Once it drops to this temperature, stir

until the syrup is soft and pliable and pour or pack into molds. When cool, poured candies will have a glazed surface.

- **Hard Maple Sugar Candy.** Boil the syrup to 240°F to 242°F (or 28°F to 30°F above the boiling point.) Keep at least 1½-inches of liquid in the pan to avoid scorching. Allow to cool to 150°F and pour or pack into molds.

- **Jack Wax or Maple-on-Snow.** Kids will love this one! Start out by filling a pan with clean snow or shaved ice and keep frozen. The boiling range is wide for this treat: at the low end of 230°F (or 18°F above

the boiling point) you'll get a taffy-like candy while at the high end of 252°F (or 40°F above the boiling point) you'll have a glass-like candy. Consistency changes within this temperature range. Once your syrup has reached your preferred temperature, immediately pour it in ribbons on the snow or ice. It will be done instantly and is typically eaten right away, as it does not keep well.

- **Maple Butter or Maple Cream.** Add ¼ teaspoon of butter, cream, or oil (for dairy-free) to approximately 2 cups of pure maple syrup and boil to 236°F (or 24°F over the boiling point.) While it's boiling, fill a large bowl with ice and water. When the batch reaches the proper temperature, set the entire pot in the ice bath – do not stir or let water lap over edge. When it's cooled to room temperature, remove from the ice bath and stir slowly with a wooden spoon until it turns opaque and becomes the consistency of peanut butter. Store in the refrigerator.

Note that not all syrups will work for maple cream – light colored syrups work best.

Search online or visit your local library for more delicious maple syrup recipes – it can be used in every dish from breakfast to cocktail hour to dinner. Experiment with your recipes until you find the right consistency and don't forget to share with your friends!

Recipes

Whole Wheat Pancakes With Warm Maple Syrup

Ingredients:

1 1/3 cups whole wheat flour

1 1/2 tsp baking powder

1/4 tsp salt

1/4 tsp baking soda

1 egg, large

1 TB brown sugar

1 1/3 cups buttermilk

1 TB vegetable oil

Directions:

Measure flour, baking powder, salt, and baking soda into a large mixing bowl. In a separate bowl, combine egg, buttermilk, brown sugar, and oil. Pour wet ingredients into dry ingredients and stir just until moistened. Batter should be slightly lumpy. Let batter rest while you heat the pan. Lightly spray or oil your griddle and preheat over medium heat. Pour ¼ cup of batter for each pancake onto hot griddle. Flip the pancake when bubbles start to appear on the surface. Serve with warmed pure maple syrup.

Maple Granola

Recipe courtesy of http://vermontmaple.org/maple-recipes

Ingredients:

4 cups old-fashioned rolled oats (not quick cooking)

1 cup unsweetened, shredded coconut

1 cup sunflower seeds

1 cup pumpkin seeds

1 cup slivered almonds

1 cup roughly chopped pecans

½ cup extra virgin olive oil

1 cup pure maple syrup

Kosher salt

1 cup sweetened, dried cranberries

Directions:

Preheat oven to 325°F. Combine rolled oats, coconut, sunflower seeds, pumpkin seeds, almonds, and pecans in a large bowl. Pour maple syrup and olive oil into bowl and mix thoroughly. Sprinkle with a generous pinch of salt and pour mixture onto large baking sheet, spreading to create a uniform layer. Bake granola, stirring every 15-20 minutes, until it is golden brown, about 1 hour. Let cool and store in an airtight container.

Maple Bacon Brussel Sprouts

Ingredients:

   1 pound fresh or frozen brussels sprouts, cleaned and trimmed

   ½ pound bacon, fried and crumbled

   Kosher salt and pepper to taste

   1 TB grapeseed oil

   2 TB pure maple syrup

Directions:

Preheat oven to 400°F. Gently toss brussels sprouts with grapeseed oil and spread out in a shallow pan. Season to taste with salt and pepper. Roast on middle rack for approximately 25 minutes. Remove from oven, sprinkle with cooked bacon, and drizzle with maple syrup. Cook for an additional 5 to 10 minutes until caramelized.

Maple Mashed Sweet Potatoes

Recipe adapted from the USDA, SNAP-Ed Connection (www.recipefinder.nal. usda.gov/recipes)

Ingredients:

   2 sweet potatoes (large)

   2 TB plain Greek yogurt

   1 TB maple syrup

   1 TB orange juice

Directions:

Scrub potatoes and prick skin with a fork. Microwave on high for 3 to 4 minutes until soft. Scoop out the pulp into a medium bowl and mash. Stir in remaining ingredients and microwave for 1 to 2 minutes to heat through.

Maple Glazed Chicken Breasts

Recipe courtesy of www.recipes.millionhearts.hhs.gov/recipes

Ingredients:

2 TB pure maple syrup

1 TB reduced-sodium soy sauce

2 tsp lemon juice

1 clove garlic, minced

1 tsp minced fresh ginger

1/4 tsp freshly ground pepper

2 boneless, skinless chicken breasts

Directions:

Whisk syrup, soy sauce, lemon juice, garlic, ginger and pepper in a small, shallow dish. Add chicken and turn to coat with the marinade; cover and refrigerate for 2 hours, turning once. Coat an indoor grill pan with cooking spray and heat over medium heat. Remove the chicken from the marinade (reserving the marinade) and cook until an instant-read thermometer inserted into the thickest part of the breast registers 165°F, 3 to 5 minutes per side.

Meanwhile, pour the reserved marinade into a small saucepan and bring to a simmer over medium heat. Cook until reduced by about half, about 4 minutes. Liberally baste the chicken with the reduced sauce and serve.

Maple Caramel Sauce

This recipe was served at President Obama's 2013 Inaugural Luncheon. Recipe courtesy of www.inaugural.senate.gov/luncheon/recipe

Ingredients:

4 oz. butter

1 cup light brown sugar, packed

Pinch of salt

½ cup pure maple syrup

Directions:

In a small saucepan over medium-high heat, melt butter. Add sugar and salt. Cook, stirring constantly, until sugar is completely dissolved, then adjust heat to medium and boil 2 minutes longer. Add maple syrup and boil, stirring frequently, until sauce is thick, smooth, and coats a spoon, 2 to 4 minutes longer. Remove from heat and hold warm for serving. Pour over ice cream, pound cake, oatmeal, or fruit crisp.

Smoky Mustard-Maple Salmon

Recipe courtesy of www.choosemyplate.gov/healthy-eating-tips/sample-menus-recipes

Ingredients:

> 3 TB whole-grain or Dijon mustard
>
> 1 TB pure maple syrup
>
> 1/4 tsp smoked paprika or ground chipotle pepper
>
> 1/4 tsp freshly ground pepper
>
> 1/8 tsp salt
>
> 4 4-oz skinless, center-cut, wild-caught salmon fillets

Directions:

Preheat oven to 450°F degrees. Line a baking sheet with foil and coat with cooking spray. Combine mustard, maple syrup, paprika (or chipotle), pepper, and salt in a small bowl. Place salmon fillets on the prepared baking sheet. Spread the mustard mixture evenly on the salmon. Roast until just cooked through (approx. 8-12 minutes).

CHAPTER SIX

Additional Resources

W e've packed this book full of information and there's lots more to learn! With such an historical but still-thriving industry, there are hundreds of fantastic resources out there to help you learn more about sugarmaking. You might want to check the following resources for more information. Don't forget, of course, the two best resources available: your local library and other sugarmakers in your area!

Books and Publications

Tree identification:

- *Smithsonian Handbook: Trees* by Allen Coombes
- *Identifying Maple Trees for Syrup Production* by C. Vogt. Fact Sheet #6286: University of Minnesota Extension

History:

- *Sweet Maple: Life, Lore & Recipes from the Sugarbush* by Paul Boisvert
- *Science of Sap: Eating the Sun: How Plants Power the Planet* by Oliver Morton

Recipes:

- *Modern Maple* by Teresa Marrone

Children's Books:

- *A Kid's Guide to Maple Tapping* by Julie Fryer
- *Living Sunlight: How Plants Bring the Earth to Life* by Molly Bang

Websites and Organizations

Begin your research locally and search for your state's "maple producers" association. These groups typically host meetings and group learning sessions where you can tag along with a professional sugarmaker.

Check, too, with your State's Extension Services, University, or Department of Agriculture. Often, these public institutions have experts on hand to answer questions or provide assistance. We found great info at these sites:

University of Vermont at http://www.uvm.edu/extension/maple/

Cornell University Cooperative Extension at maple.dnr.cornell.edu

University of Minnesota Extension Service at www.extension.umn.edu

University of Maine at umaine.edu

Look for learning days at Nature Centers or State Parks. Most offer maple season tapping days or maple syrup festivals that give families a hands-on chance to tap a tree and help with making syrup. Search for "maple tapping events" in your area.

Check out supplier websites for more info on individual tapping products or syrup making supplies. Our website can be found at www.mapletapper.com – we have blogs and video links explaining the entire tapping process in addition to a great Q & A section that gives you the opportunity to submit your own question. We also have the preassembled tapping kits available on our site and they can be found by clicking on the links at the front of this book.

CHAPTER SEVEN

A Few Final Notes

We're so glad we've been able to share the world of sugarmaking with you and we hope this book will be helpful as you continue from season to season. We know you'll quickly become an expert and soon be looking for more trees to tap! Good luck in the woods and thank you for spending a little time with us to learn a new hobby.

A Little Bit about the Sugarmakers who Helped with this Book

We'd like to take a moment to thank the folks who so kindly allowed us to tap their trees, pick their brains, and get in the way while they were making syrup! We could not have written this book without this amazing group of people. Thank you!

Chantel and Ken Prigge, owners of The Granary. Chantel, her husband, and their five children live in southeastern Minnesota where they manage a hobby farm and fruit and vegetable garden, all while Chantel runs the household and homeschools the kids and Ken works in construction. Each spring they run nearly 200 taps, continuously working on their batches and bottling them up for sale at local growers' markets. They love sugaring because it gets them outside in the early spring as the whole family works together. Chantel can be reached at cnprigge@gmail.com.

Jason and Alesha Worden. The Wordens live on a small farm in Southeastern Minnesota where they're raising three rambunctious boys. They graciously allowed the author and her husband access to their stand of maple trees and shared in the experience of tapping trees. It was a first for them! With their three boys' assistance, we gathered a few gallons of sap and ended up with enough syrup for a pancake breakfast. They're looking forward to continuing this hobby for seasons to come.

Dennis Barth. Dennis runs an excavating business in southern Minnesota and owns many acres of forested land. He also shared his maple trees for the making of the book asking only for an apple pie and some syrup in return!

Bob and Jean Fryer. In-laws to the author, Bob and Jean live on the outskirts of Lanesboro, Minnesota, and have tapped trees and made syrup for years – including a try at box elder syrup. From the start of this book, they submitted to her many questions and were happy to share all they've learned as home hobbyists.

Allan Herrmann, Owner of Hermann's Maple Syrup. During the 2014 season, Al tapped over 1800 maple trees and continues to run the maple syrup business started by his father. As a large commercial producer, Al uses advanced methods including vacuum tube collection, reverse osmosis processing techniques, and press filtering. His advice is to find other sugarmakers and learn from them as most are happy to share their experience. Al can be reached at mapleal@dbwireless.net or by mail at W1001 Lindgrin Road; Colby, WI 54421.

A Little Bit About the Author

Julie Fryer is an experienced non-fiction gardening and hobbyist writer and has published numerous books, articles, and blogs including "The Complete Guide to Your New Root Cellar," and "The Teen's Ultimate Guide to Making Money When You Can't Get a Job." She lives in a small Southeastern Minnesota town where she keeps a large veggie, herb, and flower garden. Julie and her husband's extended family have tapped maple trees on his father's land and have even tried making box elder syrup – everyone agrees maple is best! She's also assisted in the boiling down process including splitting and stacking the wood prior to the season. When she's not out gardening or cooking up her bounty, she can be found camping in the blufflands, fishing local trout streams, or out scouring flea markets for treasures.

A Little Bit About the Publisher

As a young boy, Jim Kuehnle tapped maple trees with his Grandfather in the woods of their Michigan farm. Continuing that tradition with his own children led him to start a maple tapping supply business called Maple Tapper (www.mapletapper.com). In addition to this business, Jim runs the Illinois-based chain of retail garden shops called Clover's Garden Center (www.cloversgardencenter.com). Clover's has multiple retail outlets as well as an online store. A main focus of both businesses is to encourage people to get outside and to get back in touch with nature. Jim is pleased to bring this beginner's guide for those looking to get started with the nature-centered activity of maple tapping. In addition to this book, Clover's also has available online ebooks about growing peppers, growing heirloom tomatoes, and many helpful gardening related articles.

Bibliography

Blumenstock, Marvin (author); Hopkins, Kathy (editor); How to Tap Maple Trees and Make Maple Syrup, 2007, www.umaine.edu/publications/7036e/

Bower, Jackie, Tapping Birch Trees, March 23, 2007, University of New Hampshire Cooperative Extension

Cornell Sugar Maple Research & Extension Program, Frequently Asked Questions for the Maple Producer, Forest Owner, and Consumer, authored by Peter J. Smallidge, Marianne E. Krasny, Lewis J. Staats, Steve Childs, and Mike Farrell, 2013, http://maple.dnr.cornell.edu/

Farrell, Michael, Producing Syrup from the Sap of Black Walnut Trees in the eastern U.S., Cornell University, http://www.extension.org/pages/71112/youtube-channel-walnut-syrup-series#.VWh2Nc9Viko

Haritan, Adam, 22 Trees than can be Tapped for Sap and Syrup, 2014, http://wildfoodism.com/2014/02/04/22-trees-that-can-be-tapped-for-sap-and-syrup/

Heiligmann, Randall B., Ohio State School of Natural Resources, Hobby Maple Syrup Production, www.ohioline.osu.edu/for-fact/0036.html

Hellferich, Deirdre, White Gold in the Boreal Forest, University of Alaska Fairbanks, http://www.uaf.edu/files/snras/MP_04_02.pdf

Lightsey, George R., Mother Earth News, How to Make Maple Syrup at Home: Use freeze concentration methods to make maple syrup at home without the mess and expense of boiling the sap., www.motherearthnews.com/real-food/how-to-make-maple-syrup-at-home, January/February 1974.

MacWelch, Tim, How to Make Sycamore Syrup, Easy and Cheap, February 10, 2014, http://www.outdoorlife.com/blogs/survivalist/2014/02/how-make-sycamore-syrup-easy-and-cheap

Massachusetts Maple Producers Association, Explaining Sap Flow, 2014, www.massmaple.org/sap.php

Michigan Maple Syrup Association, 2003, Facts and Figures, http://www.mi-maplesyrup.com/education/facts.htm

Mittman, Steve, How to Make Maple Syrup at Home, 10 Steps to Success, 2014, www.mainesugarworks.com

Nebraska Forest Service, Sugar Maple, www.nfs.unl.edu/CommunityForestry/Trees/SugarMaple.pdf

Noonan, Jacob, Black Walnut Sugaring and Tree Health, October 27, 2014, http://www.slideshare.net/jnoonan24/black-walnut-sugaring-and-tree-health

Somerset County Maple Producers Association, New Options for the Maple Spout or Spile, 2012, http://articles.dailyamerican.com/2012-09-21/magazines/34009861_1_spile-maple-producers-maple-syrup-digest

Styles, Serena, Nutrition of Pure Maple Syrup vs Honey, 2014, http://healthyeating.sfgate.com/nutrition-pure-maple-syrup-vs-honey-1756.html

United States Department of Agriculture National Agricultural Statistics Service, Maple Syrup Production, 2014, www.nass.usda.gov/Statistics_by_State/New_England_includes/Publications/0605mpl.pdf

Notes and Comments

Keep track of your own tapping experiences with this handy notes section.

Made in the USA
Monee, IL
27 September 2023

43464576R00056